Contents

What are fairgrounds?	4
Rides and games	6
Fairgrounds in the past	8
All the fun of the fair	10
Fairgrounds around the world	12
Fairground art and music	14
Science in fairgrounds	16
Strange sensations	18
Make a carousel	20
Fairground people	22
Zoah's story	24
Fairground safety	26
Facts and figures	28
Glossary	30
Further reading and websites	31
Index	32

What are fairgrounds?

Fairgrounds are places where people go to have fun. You can enjoy all sorts of rides at a fairground, from a fast and scary rollercoaster to a gentle carousel. You can also play fairground games and buy snacks and drinks from stalls.

Fairgrounds look amazing at night, when all the rides are lit up.

Different fairgrounds

Many fairgrounds are temporary. These fairgrounds are public spaces, such as parks, where a travelling fair can visit. Other fairgrounds are permanent. They are home to a funfair that stays open all year round. Permanent fairgrounds are often known as amusement parks. They have bigger rides than temporary fairgrounds and they cover a larger area.

Explore!
FAIRGROUNDS

Jane Bingham

WAYLAND

Published in 2015 by Wayland

Copyright © Wayland 2015

Wayland
338 Euston Road
London NW1 3BH

Wayland Australia
Level 17/207 Kent Street
Sydney, NSW 2000

Editors: Victoria Brooker and Julia Adams
Designer: Elaine Wilkinson
Picture Researcher: Shelley Noronha
Illustrations: Peter Bull

British Library Cataloguing in Publication Data

Fairgrounds. -- (Explore!)
1. Amusement parks--Juvenile literature.
I. Series
791'.068-dc23

First published in 2012 by Wayland

ISBN 978 0 7502 8406 6

Printed in China

Wayland is a division of Hachette Children's
Books, an Hachette UK company

www.hachette.co.uk

Picture acknowledgements:
The author and publisher would like to thank the
following agencies and people for allowing these
pictures to be reproduced:

p. 8: Hulton Archive/Getty Images; p. 9 (top):
Russell Lee/Buyenlarge/Getty Images; p. 9
(bottom): DEA/G. DAGLI ORT; p. 10: www.
picturethepast.org.uk/Nottingham City Council/
HIP/TopFoto; p. 11 (top): STARSTOCK/
Photoshot; p. 11 (bottom): Curt Teich Postcard
Archives/HIP/TopFoto; p. 12: Dreamstime;
p. 13 (top): Ilpo Musto/Rex Features; p. 15 (top):
Imagebrokers/Photoshot; p. 15 (bottom): EE
Images/HIP/TopFoto; p. 19 (top): Corbis Flirt/
Alamy; p. 19 (bottom): Angie Knost/Alamy;
p. 22: Fox Photos/Getty Images; p. 23 (top):
Harry Todd/Fox Photos/Getty Images; p. 23
(bottom): Rex Features; p. 24: Matt Powers/
SWNS; p. 25: Andrew Dunn/Alamy; p. 26:
UPPA/Photoshot; p. 27 (top): Carl Purcell
All other images and creative graphics:
Shutterstock

Please note:
The website addresses (URLs) included in this book were
valid at the time of going to press. However, because of the
nature of the Internet, it is possible that some addresses
may have changed, or sites may have changed or closed
down since publication. While the author and publishers
regret any inconvenience this may cause to the readers,
no responsibility for any such changes can be accepted by
either the author or the publishers.

Traditional rides

Funfairs offer rides to suit all kinds of people. Some people enjoy thrill rides, like the rollercoaster (see page 16). Others prefer traditional rides, such as the carousel or the swing boats. Carousels and swing boats have been part of the fun of the fair for over 200 years. Riders on a carousel sit on painted horses that move slowly round in a circle, rising gently up and down as they go. Swing boats hang from a high frame and are worked by the riders pulling on a rope.

Carousel horses are decorated with traditional patterns.

High rides

Most fairgrounds have a Ferris wheel and a helter skelter. The Ferris wheel has seats, called gondolas, hanging down from it. The wheel turns slowly, and riders at the top of the wheel have an amazing view. The helter skelter ride is a tall tower. Riders sit on mats and race down a long slide that circles around the tower.

Ferris wheels have a long history. The first wheel was built in Chicago in 1893.

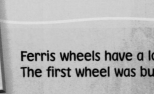

Rides and games

Some people love the speed and excitement of a thrill ride, such as the rollercoaster. Other people prefer to try their skill at a fairground game. You can also enjoy amazing sideshows at a fair, such as the hall of mirrors, where you walk past a series of mirrors that change your shape and size.

Extreme thrills

New rides are constantly being invented to create more extreme thrills. In the Frisbee ride, seats are arranged in a circle on a disc that looks like a giant frisbee. The Frisbee is attached to a long arm, that spins around very fast. Another extreme ride is the Booster. It has a very long arm mounted on a high pole, with seats at either end, and the arm spins around in an enormous circle. At its top speed, the Booster spins at a rate of 13 times a minute.

You need very strong nerves to ride the Booster!

In this game, people try to throw a ball into one of the clowns' open mouths. It is much harder than it looks!

Games

Fairground games give you the chance to try out your skill and win prizes. You can throw a ball through a hoop, shoot at a target, or test your strength by striking a pad with a hammer. Other popular games are 'hoopla' and 'hook the duck'. Some fairs have a coconut shy. In this traditional game, people throw wooden balls at coconuts and try to knock them off their stands.

Sideshows

Many fairs have sideshows, where you can marvel at surprising sights. The haunted house and the hall of mirrors are two very popular sideshows. In the haunted house, you see spooky figures, hear weird noises, and feel ghostly fingers brushing against your face!

Haunted house sideshows are especially scary at night.

Fairgrounds in the past

The history of fairgrounds dates back to the Middle Ages. In the 1200s, merchants in Europe met in towns and cities to trade goods. These fairs were held every year, and many people came to see what was on sale. Entertainers put on shows to amuse the crowds, and there were food stalls selling hot pies.

Bartholomew Fair in London began in the twelfth century. This picture shows the fair in the 1800s.

Medieval fairs

People at a medieval fair could enjoy a range of entertainments. Musicians, jesters and jugglers all performed for the crowds, in return for a small payment. There were also skilled acrobats, who walked on stilts and balanced on tightropes. Young men who came to the fair took part in archery contests and wrestling matches.

Cattle fairs

In the USA, funfairs had their origins in cattle fairs. Cattle fairs were huge animal markets that began in the 1700s. Farmers gathered at cattle fairs to buy and sell cattle, horses, and other farm animals. Cattle fairs were also known as county fairs or state fairs, and they soon became places where people could enjoy a good day out. Just like fairs in Europe, they had food stalls, entertainments and games.

Some American county fairs were very small. This photograph dates from 1940 and shows the Delta County Fair, in Colorado.

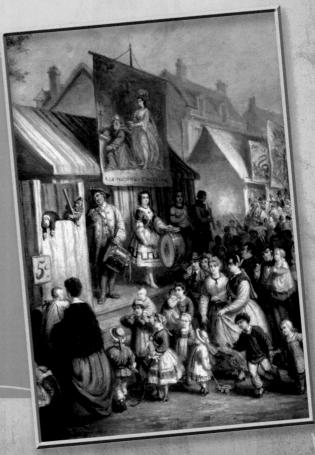

Travelling fairs

By the 1800s, funfairs had developed into a separate form of entertainment. Some fairs were still linked to trading or cattle fairs, but others were simply places to have fun. Funfairs were run by professional showmen (see pages 22-23). They were held in the same place every year, and they usually lasted for about a week. At the end of the week, all the fairground equipment was packed up. Then it was transported to the next fairground on carts pulled by horses.

Professional entertainers delight the crowds at a winter fair in France in the 1800s.

All the fun of the fair

Fairs in the 1800s had a few simple rides, such as a carousel and a set of swing boats. There were many sideshows, held in tents or wooden kiosks (huts). Fairgoers could pay to watch a play or a puppet show. There were also displays of wild animals, and showmen performed tricks such as fire-eating.

Steam power

The early carousels were turned by a team of ponies or boys. Then in the 1860s, carousels with steam engines were developed. These new, steam-powered rides could be much larger and more elaborate than before. At the same time, steam-driven fairground organs began to replace musicians and singers.

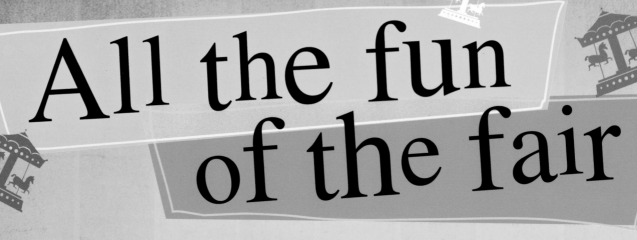

Electric rides

By the 1900s, most fairground rides were driven by powerful electric motors. This new development allowed engineers to invent some exciting new rides. Many new rides were created in the first half of the twentieth century, including the dodgems and the waltzer (a ride where cars move round a circular rack that rises up and down while the cars spin around).

These girls from the 1950s are enjoying a waltzer ride. The first waltzer ride was built in 1933.

Luna Park, Coney Island, N. Y.

Amusement parks

In the 1870s, people began to build very large fairgrounds that stayed open all year round. These permanent fairgrounds were known as amusement parks. One of the most exciting early amusement parks was Luna Park at Coney Island, New York, USA. When it opened, in 1903, people were amazed to see the whole fairground lit up with electric lights.

A postcard from 1916 showing Luna Park, in New York City, full of people having a great day out.

Fairgrounds around the world

There are millions of fairgrounds all over the world, and each one has its own character. Cedar Point, Ohio, was opened in 1870 and is one of the oldest amusement parks in the USA. It has 74 rides, including 16 rollercoasters. Saint Giles' Fair has been held in the streets of Oxford, England, for over 800 years. When the fair is in town, Oxford city centre is closed to traffic.

The Prater is one of Vienna's most famous sights, and it looks especially good at night.

The Vienna Prater

The Vienna Prater is held in a park in Vienna, the capital city of Austria. The Prater lasts from March to October, although a few rides stay open all year round. The best-known ride in the Prater is the giant Ferris wheel, but the park has many other attractions, including a ghost train, a bowling alley and an exhibition of waxwork figures (similar to Madame Tussauds).

Dancers entertain the crowds at the Sonepur Mela, in India. The fair sometimes lasts for a whole month.

The Sonepur Mela

The Sonepur Mela is held on the banks of the River Ganges, in India. This enormous fair takes place every November and includes a parade of decorated elephants. The fair began when traders met to sell elephants. Nowadays, it is forbidden to sell elephants, but animals for sale include horses, buffaloes and goats. Jugglers, magicians, singers and dancers entertain the crowds and stallholders sell handmade tools, furniture, toys, clothing and jewellery.

Fairground food around the world

Each country has its own traditional fairground food. In Holland, people eat poffertjes – sweet cakes made from batter. French fairgoers enjoy very thin pancakes called crêpes. German fairground snacks include gingerbread figures, roasted almonds and smoked sausages. British and American fairground stalls sell hot dogs and candy floss (known in the USA as cotton candy).

Toffee apples are a popular fairground snack in the UK and the USA.

Fairground art and music

Art and music play a very important part in the total experience of going to a fair. Fairground artists use vivid colours, dramatic images and bold lettering. Fairground music is played very loudly, and it usually has a powerful beat.

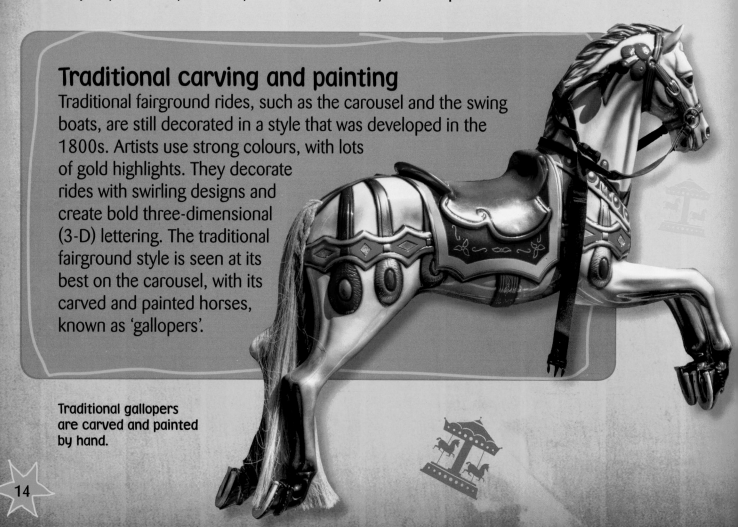

Traditional carving and painting

Traditional fairground rides, such as the carousel and the swing boats, are still decorated in a style that was developed in the 1800s. Artists use strong colours, with lots of gold highlights. They decorate rides with swirling designs and create bold three-dimensional (3-D) lettering. The traditional fairground style is seen at its best on the carousel, with its carved and painted horses, known as 'gallopers'.

Traditional gallopers are carved and painted by hand.

Modern styles

In the 1980s, a new style of art was introduced into fairgrounds. Artists painted very realistic, air-brushed figures and scenes. Around the same time, moulded plastic took over from carved wood. Today's fairground artists use styles and images that are copied from popular films, computer games and comics. Fairground artists also use coloured, flashing lights to create dramatic effects.

Modern fairground artists can create life-like designs. This scary figure is part of a ghost train ride.

Fairground sounds

Fairground organs were first developed in the 1880s. Early fairground organs were driven by steam. They were beautifully decorated with carved figures, and they played folk tunes and popular songs. By the 1930s, most fairground organs had been replaced by electrical sound systems. Today, powerful amplifiers pump out the latest pop tunes and thrill rides have their own dramatic sound effects. But traditional fairground organ music is still played to riders on the carousel.

This beautifully decorated fairground organ was made in France in the early twentieth century.

Science in fairgrounds

You can see science in action when you visit a fairground. The next four pages explain the science behind some popular fairground rides.

Rollercoaster cars do not have a motor. Instead, they rely on forces to keep them travelling along their track.

Rollercoaster forces

A force is a form of energy, such as a push or a pull, that acts on an object to make it move or to make it slow down and stop. Forces include gravity, which pulls things down to Earth, and friction, which makes moving things slow down and stop. When an object has been pushed or pulled, it develops momentum. Momentum keeps an object travelling in the same direction until the force of friction makes it stop. All these forces are at work in a rollercoaster ride.

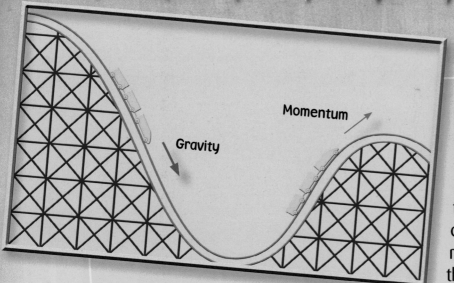

Momentum

Gravity

Gravity and momentum

At the start of a rollercoaster ride, the cars are pulled up to their starting point by a chain or a cable. When they have reached this very high point, they rely on the force of gravity to pull them down the slope very fast. As the cars speed down the slope, their momentum increases, and this momentum is strong enough to push them all the way up the next slope. Once the cars have reached the top of the second slope, the force of gravity starts to work on them again. They plunge downwards very fast and their momentum carries them up the next slope. This process continues until the ride ends.

Friction at work

Friction between the wheels of the rollercoaster cars and the track control the speed of the cars. At the end of the ride, the brakes on the car wheels are applied. Friction between the wheels and the track make the cars slow down and come to a stop.

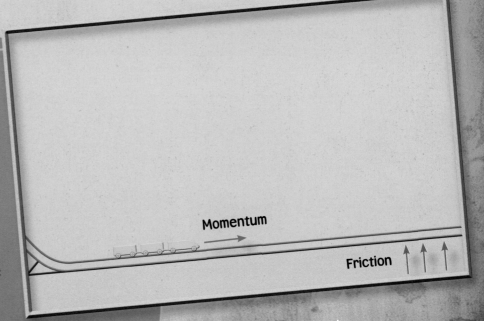

Momentum

Friction

Strange sensations

Riders on a rollercoaster experience some strange physical sensations (feelings). As they rise up rapidly, their bodies feel very heavy. When they reach the top of a rise, they feel almost weightless. These physical effects are caused by the forces of gravity and momentum working on the body.

Ups and downs

When a rollercoaster car travels upwards very fast, the force of the car pushing against riders from behind combines with the pull of gravity to make them feel heavy and forced back into their seats. At the top of the rise, the upward momentum of the riders continues although the car is beginning to go down. At this point, riders experience negative gravity. This makes them feel weightless and they have the sensation that they could fly up into the sky.

When you ride on a rollercoaster, you feel some powerful forces at work on your body.

Sticking to the sides

Have you ever tried to spin a bucket of water round very fast? The spinning movement makes the water seem to push against the sides of the bucket, when in fact the sides of the bucket are pushing against the water. This is called the centripetal effect. Some fairground attractions use the centripetal effect to create an exciting experience for the riders.

You can see the centripetal effect at work when you swing a bucket of water round very fast.

The centripetal effect makes the people on this ride stick to the sides of the drum.

Centripetal rides

Riders on the Rotor and Gravitron begin the ride by standing with their backs against a large circular drum. Then the drum starts to spin very fast. As the drum gathers speed, the floor beneath the riders' feet slowly drops away, but the riders do not fall. The centripetal effect makes their bodies stick to the sides of the drum.

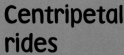

Make a carousel

This model carousel can be turned by pulling on a cotton thread. If you use a thread that doesn't show up too much, people will think the carousel is turning by itself!

1 Place a small plate on the sheet of card and draw around it. Cut out your circular roof shape and colour it. Use the points of your scissors to make four small holes, as shown.

2 Make a cut as shown. Glue the shaded section to the underside of your carousel roof. This will make a sloping roof.

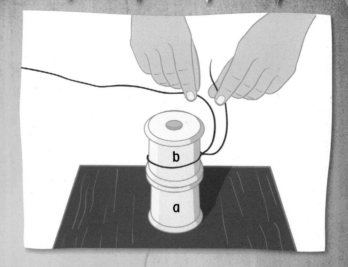

3 Draw four horse shapes on card. Cut them out and colour the horses on both sides. Next, make a small hole in the back of each horse. Thread equal lengths of cord through each of the holes and tie the horses to the holes in the carousel roof.

4 Glue cotton reel (a) onto the wooden base and wait for it to dry. Tie the cotton thread (about 50 cm long) around cotton reel (b). If the thread slips, fix it in place with sticky tape. Stand cotton reel (b) on top of cotton reel (a).

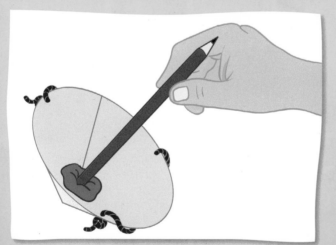

5 Stick the flat end of the pencil into a small lump of modelling clay. Push the clay into the inside top of the carousel roof. Pass the pencil's pointed end through reel (b) and halfway through reel (a). Now pull on the cotton thread and watch your carousel turn around!

Fairground people

People who run travelling fairs are also called 'showmen'. From around April to October, showmen move from place to place. They travel with trucks (to carry their equipment) and caravans (where they sleep and cook their meals). At each place they visit, they spend a day setting up their rides, shows and stalls. After running the fair for a few days, they pack everything away and move on to the next place.

Fairground families

Most fairground families have been running fairs for many generations. Children start helping their parents at a very young age, and most of them work on fairs when they grow up. Boys and girls from fairground families usually marry partners from the showman community.

This photograph, taken in 1934, shows a fairground child, his father and grandfather at their family coconut shy.

Showman slang

Travelling showmen have close links with the Romani (gypsy) people. They have a special slang that includes many words from the Romani language. Showmen use the words 'flatty' and 'joskin' to describe a person who does not belong to the showman community.

Showmen at work, constructing a rollercoaster ride in 1933.

This fairground family have spent the winter months restoring their rides.

A travelling life

Fairground people live in caravans or mobile homes. In the spring, summer and autumn, they are constantly on the move. In the winter, they live in a caravan park that they call their 'winter yard'. During the winter months, the children go to school near their winter yard. While they are travelling, fairground children keep in touch with their school teachers and follow distance-learning courses.

Zoah's story

Zoah Hedges-Stocks spent her childhood working on fairgrounds. Then, at the age of 19, she won a place to study history at Cambridge University. Here, Zoah talks about growing up in a fairground family.

Zoah wearing her Cambridge student's gown.

Q Have your family always worked on fairgrounds?

A My family have been travelling showmen for about 200 years. My mum runs a food kiosk, selling burgers, toffee apples and candy floss. My uncle runs a dodgems ride, which he took over from my grandad. When I was little, I loved to listen to Grandad's stories of fairground life. That's how I first got interested in history.

Q What was it like to be always on the move?

A I had the same routine every year. In the winter, I lived in a mobile home in a small town in Suffolk, and I went to school down the road. In the summer, I travelled all over the east of England, working on different fairgrounds. Sometimes, I felt really tired after a long day's work, but I always liked the fun of waking up in a new place. Now I miss the experience of sleeping in a caravan. I love the sound of rain on a caravan roof.

Q How did you manage to keep up with your schoolwork?

A Until I was 15, I always missed the summer term at school. But I kept on reading and learning all the time. Fairgrounds are a good place to learn about life and I learnt maths by giving change on the kiosk.

Q How did you get on with the other children at school?

A At first, I was teased by the other children because my life was so different from theirs. But I soon learnt to stick up for myself. I know where I come from and I'm proud of it. Travellers have a very strong sense of family, unity and loyalty.

The Midsummer Fair in Cambridge was one of the highlights of Zoah's year when she was growing up. She worked at the fair in Cambridge for a week each summer. But she never guessed that sometime in the future, she would be a student at Cambridge University.

Fairground safety

How safe are fairgrounds? In the past there were some tragic accidents, but most fairgrounds today have an excellent safety record. Organisers of travelling fairs need to meet some very strict safety standards before they are allowed to hold a fair.

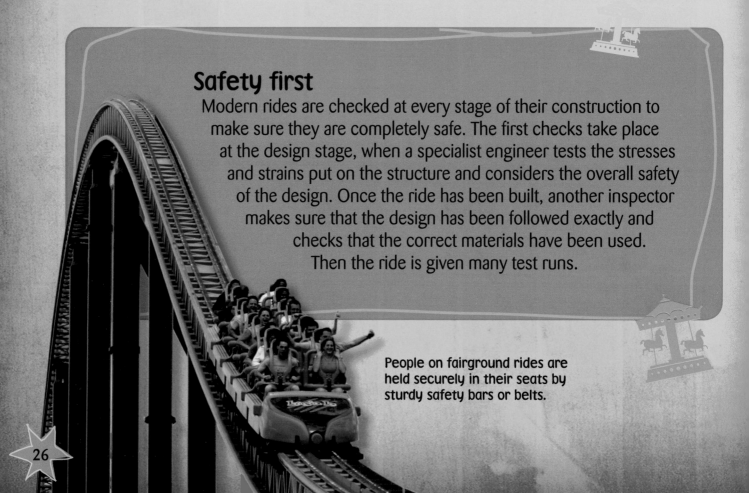

Safety first

Modern rides are checked at every stage of their construction to make sure they are completely safe. The first checks take place at the design stage, when a specialist engineer tests the stresses and strains put on the structure and considers the overall safety of the design. Once the ride has been built, another inspector makes sure that the design has been followed exactly and checks that the correct materials have been used. Then the ride is given many test runs.

People on fairground rides are held securely in their seats by sturdy safety bars or belts.

Many tests

After a ride has passed all its test runs, it is given a daily inspection. Before the fair opens each day, the ride is checked thoroughly and all the checks and repairs are entered into an inspection book. At the end of each year, all rides have to pass an annual safety test.

This photograph shows a safety engineer checking a rollercoaster ride in 1955.

Fairground accidents

The number of fairground accidents is extremely low. In fact, you are much more likely to have an accident on a train journey than on a fairground ride. But even one fairground accident is too many. Each time there is an accident, people study what happened very carefully. They investigate the cause of the accident so they can make fairgrounds safer places to be.

There are strict rules about the height that a child must be before he or she is allowed on a thrill ride. There must be no danger that a child could slip out of a harness that is too big.

Facts and figures

The world's tallest rollercoaster track is Kingda Ka at Six Flags Great Adventure in Jackson, New Jersey, USA. At its highest point it is 139 m (456 ft) tall.

Formula Rossa at Ferrari World in Abu Dhabi, United Arab Emirates, is the fastest rollercoaster ride in the world. The rollercoaster cars reach a top speed of 240 km/h (150 mph). After the cars leave the top of the ride, they take about 4.9 seconds to reach this speed.

Steel Dragon 2000 at Nagashima Spa Land in Kuwana, Mie, Japan, is the world's longest rollercoaster track. It is 2,479 m (8,133 ft) long.

Between the years 1608 and 1814, there were some very cold winters in Britain, and around a dozen 'frost fairs' were held on the frozen River Thames. At the last frost fair, in 1814, an elephant was led across the frozen river.

The earliest known image of a fairground ride is a carving from Constantinople (modern-day Istanbul). It dates from around 500 CE and shows riders in baskets hanging from a central pole.

The first rollercoaster rides were built in Russia in the 1600s. They were tall wooden slides covered with a layer of ice, and people sat in sledges that raced down the icy slopes. The first wooden rollercoasters, with cars that travelled on tracks, were built in the early 1800s. They were known as 'Russian Mountains'.

Glossary

air-brushed Painted by using a spray gun to blow the paint onto a surface.

amplifiers Boxes that increase the volume of sounds.

amusement park A large fairground that is open all year round or for most of the year.

annual Happening every year.

archery Shooting with a bow and arrows.

attraction A show or ride that is intended to entertain people.

carousel A fairground roundabout with horses to ride on.

community A group of people who live or work close together.

dodgems A fairground ride, in which people ride small cars and crash into each other on purpose. Dodgems are also known as bumper cars.

engineer Someone who designs and checks machinery.

equipment The machines or tools that are needed to make or do something.

experience An event, happening or feeling.

Ferris wheel A very large wheel with seats attached to it, that spins around slowly.

force A form of energy, such as a push or a pull.

friction A force that makes a moving object slow down and stop.

generation People born around the same time. Grandparents, parents and children belong to three different generations.

gravity A force that pulls things down towards the surface of the Earth.

investigate To find out all about something.

kiosk A small hut or stand, where things are sold.

Middle Ages A period in history between around 1000 CE and 1450 CE.

momentum A force that keeps an object travelling in the same direction until the force of friction makes it stop.

permanent Lasting for a long time, or for ever.

showmen People who run fairs or other entertainments.

sideshow A small show to entertain people.

slang Words and phrases used by groups of people among themselves.

stalls Small huts or stands where things are sold.

temporary Lasting for a short while.

thrill rides Fast and scary rides that are designed to make people feel excited.

traditional Done in the same way for a very long time.

Further reading

BOOKS

Showfolk: An Oral History of a Fairground Dynasty (Flashbacks), Frank Bruce (NMSE Publishing, 2010) The story of a Scottish fairground family told through interviews.

Fairground Attraction, John Comino-James (Dewi Lewis Publishing, 2003) Photographs of British fairground families taken throughout the year.

Vintage Funfairs: Amusement Rides, Carousels and Fairground Art, Brian Steptoe (Jumper Books, 2002) Photographs of old fairground rides in the UK, Europe, the USA and Australia.

Websites

www.fairground-heritage.org.uk/newsite/learn/learn-home.html
An illustrated history of fairgrounds in Britain

www.glasgowsciencecentre.org/forcesatthefunfair.aspx
An interactive website that allows you to adjust the forces on a rollercoaster ride in order to change the speed of a ride.

www.bbc.co.uk/learningzone/clips/maths-at-the-fairground/6189.html
This webpage about advanced maths challenges linked to fairgrounds includes a video showing a fairground being set up.

Index

amusement parks 4, 11, 12, 30
animals 9, 10, 13, 29
art 5, 14–15
Austria 12

Bartholomew Fair 8
Booster 6
bowling alley 12

carousel 4–5, 10, 14–15,
    20–21, 30
cattle fairs 9
centripetal effect 19
coconut shy 7, 22

dodgems 11, 24, 30

education 23, 24–25
electric rides 6, 11, 19, 24
entertainers 8–9, 10, 13
equipment 9, 22, 30
Europe 8–9, 12–13, 15

fairground families 22–23,
    24–25
Ferris wheel 5, 12, 30
food and drink 4, 8–9, 13, 22,
    24
forces 16–17, 18–19, 30
Formula Rossa 28
France 9, 13, 15
friction 16–17, 30
Frisbee ride 6

games 4, 6–7, 8–9

Germany 13
ghost train 12, 15
Gravitron 19
gravity 16–17, 18, 30

hall of mirrors 6–7
haunted house 7
Hedges-Stocks, Zoah 24-25
helter skelter 5
history 8–9, 10–11
hook the duck 7
hoopla 7

India 13

Japan 28

Kingda Ka 28

Luna Park 11

Middle Ages 8
Middle East 28
Midsummer Fair 25
momentum 16–17, 18, 30
music 8, 10, 13, 14–15

organs 10, 15

permanent fairgrounds [see
    amusement parks]

rides 4–5, 6–7, 10–11, 12,
    14–15, 16–17, 18–19, 20–21,
    22–23, 24, 26–27, 28–29, 30

rollercoaster 4–5, 6, 12, 16–17,
    18, 23, 26–27, 28–29
Rotor 19
Russia 29

safety 26–27
Saint Giles' Fair 12
science 16–17, 18–19
showmen 9, 10, 22–23, 24-25,
    30
sideshows 6–7, 10, 22, 30
Sonepur Mela 13
sounds 7, 8, 10, 13, 14–15
stalls 4, 8–9, 13, 22, 30
steam-powered rides 10
Steel Dragon 2000 28
swing boats 5, 10, 14

temporary fairgrounds [see
    travelling fairgrounds]
thrill rides 4–5, 6, 11, 12, 15,
    16–17, 18–19, 23, 26–27,
    28–29, 30
trade fairs 8–9, 13
traditional rides 4–5, 10, 12,
    14–15, 20–21, 30
travelling fairgrounds 4, 9, 12,
    22–23, 24–25, 26

UK 8, 12–13, 24–25, 29
USA 5, 9, 11, 12–13, 28

Vienna Prater 12

waltzer 11